We Read
PHONICS™

Big Cats

TREASURE BAY

Parent's Introduction

Welcome to **We Read Phonics**! This series is designed to help you assist your child in reading. Each book includes a story, as well as some simple word games to play with your child. The games focus on the phonics skills and sight words your child will use in reading the story.

Here are some recommendations for using this book with your child:

1 **Word Play**

There are word games both before and after the story. Make these games fun and playful. If your child becomes bored or frustrated, play a different game or take a break.

Pat rhymes with cat.

Very good!

Phonics is a method of sounding out words by blending together letter sounds. However, not all words can be "sounded out." **Sight words** are frequently used words that usually cannot be sounded out.

② Read the Story

After some word play, read the story aloud to your child—or read the story together, by reading aloud at the same time or by taking turns. As you and your child read, move your finger under the words.

Next, have your child read the entire story to you while you follow along with your finger under the words. If there is some difficulty with a word, either help your child to sound it out or wait about five seconds and then say the word.

③ Discuss and Read Again

After reading the story, talk about it with your child. Ask questions like, "What happened in the story?" and "What was the best part?" It will be helpful for your child to read this story to you several times. Another great way for your child to practice is by reading the book to a younger sibling, a pet, or even a stuffed animal!

I liked the tigers the best!

LEVEL 1   **Level 1** focuses on simple words with short "a" and short "i" (as in *cat* and *sit*). Consonants used at this level include b, c, d, f, h, m, n, p, r, s, *and* t.

Big Cats

A We Read Phonics™ Book
Level 1
Guilded Reading Level: A

Text Copyright © 2010 by Treasure Bay, Inc.

Use of photos provided by Getty Images © 2010 and Fotosearch © 2010

Reading Consultants: Bruce Johnson, M.Ed., and Dorothy Taguchi, Ph.D.

We Read Phonics™ is a trademark of Treasure Bay, Inc.

Published by
Treasure Bay, Inc.
P.O. Box 119
Novato, CA 94948 USA

Printed in Malaysia

Library of Congress Catalog Card Number: 2009929507

Paperback ISBN: 978-1-60115-314-2

Visit us online at TreasureBayBooks.com

PR-11-20

Big Cats

By Bruce Johnson

Phonics Game

Word Tic-Tac-Toe

Writing and reading these words will help your child read the story.

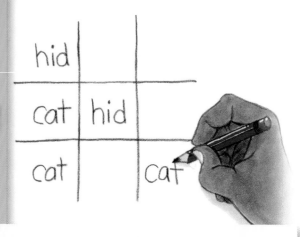

Materials needed: paper; pencils, crayons, or markers; ruler
Optional: 3 x 5 inch cards

1. Draw on the paper a traditional Tic-Tac-Toe board (a 3 x 3 grid).

2. Play this game of Tic-Tac-Toe with a twist. Instead of letters "X" and "O," players choose words from the ones listed below. For example, player 1 plays with the word *cat* and player 2 plays with the word *bad*. Player 1 says and writes the word *cat* on one of the squares, and player 2 says and writes the word *bad* on one of the squares.

3. The first player to make three in a row, across, up and down, or diagonally, wins the game.

4. If your child has difficulty writing the words, you can help her or you can write each word on five 3 x 5 cards and play using the cards.

5. Repeat the game with different words from below.

cat bad can dip sip sit fast hid nap

Words in the Room

This is a fun way to practice sight words.

1. Write each word listed on the right on a plain 3 x 5 inch card, so you have one card for each sight word. Put the cards in different parts of the room, all visible to your child.

2. Say one of the words and ask your child to find the card. If he finds the right card, he gets to keep it. If he picks the wrong card, he gives you the card. Put the card in another part of the room.

3. Keep the cards. You can combine them with other sight word cards and play a bigger version of this game. Or, if you make another set of these cards, you can play sight word games featured in other **We Read Phonics** books. (Other games require two of each card.) Play games using the words your child needs to practice.

big

see

went

be

good

this

no

go

for

See the big cat.

Cats can be good.

Cats can be bad.

Can I pat this cat? No!

See the big cat.

This cat can sit.

It can nap.

It can sip.

See the big cat.

It is fast.

Go, cat, go!

Fast, fast, fast!

See the cat.

This tan cat hid.

It went for a dip.

It nabs a rat.

See the cat.

Cats can be good.

Cats can be bad.

I can pat this cat!

Rhyming

Can you think of another word that rhymes with hid?

Kid!

Practicing rhyming words helps children learn how words are similar.

1 Explain to your child that these words rhyme because they have the same end sounds: *hid, bid, did, kid, mid, lid, rid,* and *Sid.*

2 Ask your child to say a word that rhymes with *hid.*

3 If your child has trouble, offer some possible answers or repeat step 1. It's okay to accept nonsense words, for example, *fid.*

4 When your child is successful, repeat step 2 with these words:

bad   (possible answers: *dad, fad, had, lad, mad, pad, sad*)

can   (possible answers: *ban, fan, man, pan, plan, ran, tan*)

dip   (possible answers: *flip, hip, lip, nip, rip, sip, tip*)

fast   (possible answers: *blast, cast, last, mast, past*)

nap   (possible answers: *cap, flap, lap, map, wrap, tap*)

see   (possible answers: *be, fee, free, he, key, me, she, tea, we*)

Phonics Game

Head
Waist
Toe

This is a fun way to practice breaking words into parts, which helps children learn to read new words.

1. Stand up facing your child. Make sure you have plenty of room.

2. Choose a simple three-letter word from the story.

3. Each of you touches your head for the first sound, your waist for the middle sound, and your toes for the final sound.

4. For example, for the word *nap*, say the word, repeat the word, and touch your head when saying the "n" sound, your waist when saying the short "a" sound (as in *cat*), and your toes when saying the "p" sound.

5. Continue with these additional simple three-letter words from the story: *bad, has, hat, hid, pat, rat, tap, sip,* and *nab.*

If you liked *Big Cats,*
here is another **We Read Phonics**™ book you are sure to enjoy!

Pat, Cat, and Rat

This Level 1 book is perfect for the very beginning reader. In the story, Cat wants to catch Rat and turn him into a tasty snack, but Pat is determined to prevent it! The story is simple and easy to read, and offers lots of humor that is sure to captivate young readers!